The Intuition Protocol

Breaking the Code of Subconscious Decision-Making in a Controlled World

Anthony Collins

The Intuition Protocol

Chapter 1: The Architecture of Intuitive Intelligence 5

The Evolution of Intuitive Processing............................. 5

Neuroscience of Gut Feelings 9

The Control Matrix and Intuition 13

Modern Barriers to Intuitive Flow................................ 17

The Paradox of Structured Spontaneity....................... 21

Chapter 2: The Control Systems That Shape Our Decisions... 26

Social Programming and Intuitive Suppression 26

Digital Age Interference 30

Data-Driven Decision Making vs. Intuitive Wisdom...... 34

Chapter 3: Mapping the Intuition Protocol.................. 40

Core Components of Intuitive Processing.................... 40

Breaking Through Rational Resistance......................... 44

The Role of Emotional Intelligence 48

Physical Signals and Bodily Wisdom 53

Integrating Multiple Information Streams................... 57

Chapter 4: Developing the Protocol............................. 63

Baseline Assessment Methods.................................... 63

Intuition Training Frameworks.................................... 67

Protocol Implementation Stages................................. 71

Chapter 5: Testing and Validation Methods 76

Scientific Measurement Tools 76
Experiential Documentation 80
Success Metrics 84
Real-World Application Testing 88
Protocol Refinement Processes 93
Chapter 6: Breaking Free from Control Systems 98
Identifying External Influences 98
Reclaiming Intuitive Authority 102
Environmental Optimization 106

Chapter 1: The Architecture of Intuitive Intelligence

The Evolution of Intuitive Processing

Intuitive processing has undergone a remarkable transformation throughout human history, shaped by the constant interplay between survival needs and cognitive development. Our earliest ancestors relied heavily on instantaneous gut reactions to navigate dangerous environments, make split-second decisions about food sources, and form quick judgments about potential threats or allies.

These primitive intuitive mechanisms were essential for survival, operating beneath conscious awareness through what we now understand as the limbic system. As human societies grew more complex, these basic intuitive processes evolved to handle increasingly sophisticated social interactions and environmental challenges. The ability to quickly read facial expressions, interpret social cues, and sense underlying motivations became crucial advantages in communal living.

Archaeological evidence suggests that ancient civilizations recognized and valued intuitive wisdom, often attributing it to divine inspiration or supernatural guidance. Sacred texts and philosophical writings across cultures contain numerous references to inner knowing, suggesting that our ancestors understood the importance of balancing rational thought with intuitive insight.

The medieval period marked a significant shift in how humans perceived and utilized intuition. Religious institutions began codifying knowledge and decision-making processes, gradually placing more emphasis on doctrine and rational analysis over intuitive understanding. This trend accelerated during the Enlightenment era, when scientific reasoning and empirical observation became the primary accepted paths to knowledge.

However, the industrial revolution brought unexpected challenges to human intuition. As machines replaced manual labor and standardized processes became the norm, people's natural ability to read situations and respond instinctively began to atrophy. The workplace demanded consistency and conformity rather than intuitive problem-solving, leading to a gradual suppression of these natural capabilities.

The twentieth century witnessed a fascinating paradox in intuitive processing. While scientific advancement continued to emphasize rational thinking, pioneering psychologists began documenting the crucial role of intuition in human consciousness. Carl Jung's work on the collective unconscious and intuitive archetypes opened new perspectives on how humans process information beyond rational thought.

Research in cognitive psychology has revealed that intuitive processing operates through pattern recognition at both conscious and unconscious levels. Our brains constantly scan environments for familiar patterns, comparing current situations with past experiences to generate rapid, often accurate assessments. This process happens so quickly that we experience it as a gut feeling or sudden insight rather than deliberate analysis.

Modern neuroscience has identified specific brain regions associated with intuitive processing, particularly the anterior cingulate cortex and the ventromedial prefrontal cortex. These areas integrate emotional responses with cognitive information, creating the characteristic "knowing without knowing how we know" that defines intuitive insight.

The digital age has introduced new challenges and opportunities for intuitive processing. While technology has expanded our access to information, it has also created information overload that can overwhelm our natural intuitive capabilities. Constant connectivity and digital distractions often interrupt the quiet mental space necessary for intuitive insights to emerge.

Yet paradoxically, this very challenge has sparked a renewed interest in developing and preserving intuitive abilities. Many professionals in high-stakes fields such as emergency medicine, firefighting, and business leadership actively cultivate their intuitive capabilities alongside technical expertise. They recognize that in complex, rapidly changing situations, intuition often provides crucial insights that purely analytical approaches might miss.

Recent studies in decision science have demonstrated that intuitive processing can be more accurate than detailed analysis in certain situations, particularly when dealing with complex variables or incomplete information. This finding has led to increased attention on how to preserve and enhance natural intuitive capabilities in professional training programs.

The evolution of intuitive processing continues as humans adapt to new challenges. Environmental changes, technological advancement, and social complexity create pressure for our intuitive capabilities to evolve further. Some researchers suggest that we may be developing new forms of intuition specifically adapted to digital environments and virtual interactions.

Understanding this evolutionary journey helps us appreciate both the resilience and adaptability of human intuitive processing. While our modern world often seems at odds with intuitive wisdom, the fundamental mechanisms that helped our ancestors survive continue to operate within us. By recognizing how intuitive processing has evolved and adapted throughout history, we can better understand its current manifestations and potential future developments.

The challenge now lies in consciously cultivating these natural capabilities while navigating an increasingly complex world. As we face unprecedented global challenges and rapid technological change, the ability to access and trust our evolved intuitive processing becomes more crucial than ever.

Neuroscience of Gut Feelings

Deep within the intricate networks of our brain lies a sophisticated system that generates what we commonly call gut feelings. These instinctive sensations, which often manifest as subtle physical responses or sudden knowing, are far more than simple emotional reactions. They represent the culmination of complex neurological processes that have evolved over millions of years.

The enteric nervous system, often called our "second brain," contains over 100 million neurons lining our digestive tract. This extensive neural network maintains constant communication with our brain through the vagus nerve, creating a powerful brain-gut axis that influences our decisions and emotional responses. When we experience a gut feeling, this system is actively participating in our decision-making process, drawing upon stored information and past experiences.

Research has revealed that the insula, a region of the cerebral cortex, plays a crucial role in processing these visceral signals. This area integrates sensory information from our internal organs with emotional and cognitive input, creating the physical sensations we associate with intuitive insights. When we describe having "butterflies in our stomach" or a "gut-wrenching feeling," we're experiencing the insula's interpretation of these complex neural signals.

The amygdala, our emotional processing center, works in concert with the insula to attach emotional significance to these physical sensations. This collaboration helps us recognize potential threats or opportunities before our conscious mind has time to analyze the situation fully. Studies have shown that this rapid emotional processing can occur within milliseconds, far faster than conscious deliberation.

Neuroimaging studies have revealed increased activity in the anterior cingulate cortex during moments of intuitive decision-making. This brain region helps resolve conflicts between competing sources of information and plays a vital role in error detection. When we experience a strong gut feeling, this area is often highly active, suggesting it helps integrate unconscious knowledge with conscious awareness.

The right hemisphere of our brain appears particularly important in intuitive processing. This hemisphere specializes in pattern recognition, holistic thinking, and processing non-verbal information. While the left hemisphere excels at logical analysis, the right hemisphere helps us grasp complex situations quickly and make intuitive leaps that bypass step-by-step reasoning.

Neurotransmitters also play a crucial role in gut feelings. Dopamine, often associated with reward and pleasure, spikes when we follow our intuition and achieve positive outcomes. This reinforcement helps strengthen our trust in future intuitive insights. Meanwhile, serotonin, produced both in the brain and gut, influences our emotional state and can affect the clarity of our intuitive perceptions.

The default mode network (DMN), a collection of brain regions active when we're not focused on external tasks, contributes significantly to intuitive processing. This network becomes particularly active during periods of rest or reflection, allowing our minds to process information beneath conscious awareness and generate unexpected insights.

Memory systems, particularly implicit memory, form the foundation of gut feelings. These systems store countless patterns and experiences that we've encountered throughout our lives. When we face new situations, our brains rapidly compare current circumstances with these stored patterns, generating intuitive responses based on previously learned associations.

Stress can significantly impact our ability to access these intuitive signals. Under acute stress, the prefrontal cortex's function becomes impaired, potentially disrupting our ability to interpret gut feelings accurately. However, moderate levels of stress can actually enhance intuitive processing by increasing alertness and emotional sensitivity.

The brain's plasticity allows us to strengthen these intuitive pathways through practice and attention. Regular meditation and mindfulness practices have been shown to enhance the connection between emotional and cognitive processing centers, potentially improving our ability to recognize and interpret gut feelings accurately.

Sleep plays a vital role in consolidating intuitive learning. During sleep, particularly during REM phases, our brains process and integrate experiences from the day, strengthening the neural networks that support intuitive insights. This explains why we often wake up with clear intuitive guidance after "sleeping on" a problem.

Understanding the neuroscience behind gut feelings reveals their legitimacy as a decision-making tool. These sensations aren't mysterious or magical but rather the product of sophisticated neural processes that have evolved to help us navigate complex situations. By recognizing the biological basis of intuition, we can better appreciate its value while learning to distinguish genuine intuitive insights from fear-based reactions or biased assumptions.

The challenge lies in learning to work with these natural neural mechanisms rather than against them. By cultivating awareness of our internal states and practicing regular reflection, we can enhance our ability to recognize and interpret these valuable intuitive signals effectively.

The Control Matrix and Intuition

Beneath the surface of our daily experiences lies a complex web of control systems that significantly influence our decision-making processes and intuitive capabilities. This intricate matrix operates through various societal structures, institutional frameworks, and cultural paradigms that shape our perception of reality and our trust in our inner guidance.

Educational systems form a fundamental component of this control structure, conditioning students from an early age to prioritize logical analysis over intuitive understanding. Standard curricula emphasize memorization, linear thinking, and standardized testing, effectively training young minds to doubt their natural intuitive impulses in favor of externally validated knowledge.

Media networks create another layer of control by continuously bombarding us with information, opinions, and manufactured consensus. This constant stream of external input often drowns out the subtle signals of intuitive wisdom, replacing them with pre-packaged thoughts and standardized responses to life's challenges.

Corporate environments further reinforce this matrix through rigid hierarchies and protocol-driven decision-making processes. Employees learn to suppress their intuitive insights in favor of data-driven analysis and established procedures, even when their gut feelings warn them of potential problems or opportunities.

The financial system exerts particularly powerful control over intuitive processing through its creation of artificial scarcity and competition. These conditions generate persistent anxiety and fear, emotional states that significantly impair our ability to access and trust our intuitive guidance. When survival concerns dominate our thinking, deeper intuitive wisdom often becomes inaccessible.

Social media platforms have introduced unprecedented levels of behavioral control, creating dopamine-driven feedback loops that keep users engaged while subtly directing their attention and choices. These systems exploit psychological vulnerabilities to create predictable behavior patterns, effectively bypassing our natural intuitive defenses.

Healthcare systems frequently dismiss intuitive knowledge about our own bodies, favoring standardized treatments over individualized approaches. This systematic devaluation of personal intuitive wisdom about health and healing has led many to doubt their body's natural signals and healing capabilities.

Political structures maintain control through the creation of artificial divisions and controlled narratives that prevent people from trusting their intuitive understanding of social issues. By generating constant conflict and uncertainty, these systems make it difficult to maintain the inner clarity necessary for intuitive insight.

Religious and spiritual institutions, while originally sources of intuitive wisdom, often evolve into control mechanisms that replace direct intuitive experience with prescribed beliefs and practices. This transformation from intuitive exploration to dogmatic adherence reflects a common pattern in the control matrix.

Time management in modern society serves as another control mechanism, filling our days with urgent tasks and leaving little space for the quiet reflection necessary for intuitive processing. The constant rush from one activity to another creates a state of perpetual distraction that makes accessing intuitive wisdom nearly impossible.

Consumer culture maintains its control by creating artificial needs and desires that override our intuitive sense of sufficiency and wellbeing. Marketing techniques specifically target and manipulate our emotional responses, making it difficult to distinguish between genuine intuitive guidance and manufactured wants.

Language itself functions as a subtle but powerful control mechanism, limiting our ability to express and understand intuitive experiences that often transcend verbal description. The dominance of rational, linear discourse makes it challenging to validate and share intuitive insights.

Scientific materialism, while valuable in many ways, has become another control mechanism by dismissing subjective experience and intuitive knowledge as unreliable or irrelevant. This paradigm creates a cultural bias against intuitive wisdom, even when it proves practically useful.

The technology that surrounds us introduces yet another layer of control by mediating our experience of reality through screens and algorithms. This digital filter often disconnects us from the direct, embodied experience necessary for clear intuitive perception.

Understanding these control mechanisms represents the first step toward reclaiming our intuitive capabilities. By recognizing how various systems influence our perception and decision-making, we can begin to create space for authentic intuitive guidance to emerge.

Breaking free from this control matrix requires conscious effort and practice. It involves cultivating awareness of these influences while developing strategies to maintain intuitive clarity despite external pressures. This might include creating regular periods of digital disconnection, practicing mindful awareness, and consciously questioning inherited beliefs and assumptions.

The path to intuitive freedom doesn't require complete withdrawal from these systems, but rather a balanced approach that allows us to participate in society while maintaining our intuitive sovereignty. By understanding the nature of the control matrix, we can navigate it more consciously, using our intuitive wisdom to guide us through its complexities while avoiding its traps.

Modern Barriers to Intuitive Flow

The rapid pace of contemporary life has erected numerous obstacles that block our natural intuitive flow, creating unprecedented challenges for accessing our inner wisdom. These barriers, both subtle and obvious, have fundamentally altered how we connect with our intuitive capabilities.

Digital distraction stands as perhaps the most pervasive barrier, constantly interrupting the delicate process of intuitive insight. The average person checks their phone over 100 times daily, each glance breaking the continuous thread of awareness necessary for deep intuitive connection. These micro-interruptions fragment our attention and prevent the mind from entering the receptive state required for intuitive processing.

Information overload similarly overwhelms our natural filtering systems. The human brain, evolved to process the limited information available in natural environments, now faces a tsunami of data that drowns out the subtle signals of intuition. When bombarded with excessive information, our minds default to surface-level processing, unable to access the deeper wisdom that intuition provides.

The cult of busy-ness presents another significant barrier, as modern society equates constant activity with productivity and worth. This perpetual motion leaves no space for the stillness that intuition requires. Like a pond that needs calm waters to reflect clearly, our minds need periods of quiet to receive intuitive insights.

Environmental disconnection has severed many people from the natural rhythms that traditionally supported intuitive awareness. Confined to artificial environments, surrounded by synthetic materials and artificial lighting, we've lost touch with the natural cues that once helped calibrate our intuitive senses.

Social media algorithms create echo chambers that reinforce existing beliefs and biases, making it difficult to distinguish between genuine intuitive insights and conditioned responses. These platforms also foster comparison and competition, generating anxiety that further blocks intuitive flow.

The dominance of analytical thinking in education and professional settings has created a cultural bias against intuitive knowledge. From early schooling onward, we're trained to distrust gut feelings and rely solely on logical analysis, effectively atrophying our intuitive capabilities through disuse.

Chronic stress, endemic in modern society, triggers constant fight-or-flight responses that override our subtler intuitive faculties. Under stress, blood flow diverts from the brain regions responsible for intuitive processing to those handling immediate survival responses, physically impeding our access to intuitive wisdom.

Sleep deprivation, affecting millions globally, significantly impairs intuitive function. During sleep, our brains process and integrate experiences, strengthening the neural networks that support intuitive insights. Without adequate rest, these vital processes remain incomplete, leaving us disconnected from our intuitive guidance.

The prevalence of processed foods and environmental toxins creates physical barriers to intuitive flow by disrupting the gut-brain axis. Research shows that poor gut health directly impacts cognitive function and emotional processing, both crucial components of intuitive awareness.

Electromagnetic pollution from wireless technologies may interfere with the body's natural biorhythms, potentially disrupting the subtle energetic fields through which intuitive information often travels. While research in this area remains ongoing, many report decreased sensitivity to intuitive signals in electromagnetically dense environments.

Social conditioning against emotional expression creates psychological barriers to intuitive flow. Since intuition often manifests through emotional and bodily sensations, the suppression of emotional awareness effectively blocks intuitive signals.

Time scarcity, whether real or perceived, generates a constant sense of urgency that prevents the deep listening required for intuitive insight. When racing against the clock, we default to quick, superficial decisions rather than allowing intuitive wisdom to emerge naturally.

The monetization of attention has created an economy that profits from keeping people distracted and disconnected from their inner guidance. Streaming services, social media, and entertainment platforms deliberately design their interfaces to override natural attention spans and keep users engaged in surface-level activities.

Fear-based media coverage generates chronic anxiety that blocks intuitive flow by keeping the nervous system in a state of high alert. This persistent background stress makes it difficult to access the calm, receptive state necessary for intuitive processing.

Consumer culture creates artificial desires that drown out genuine intuitive needs, replacing authentic inner guidance with manufactured wants. The constant bombardment of advertising messages disrupts our natural ability to discern what truly serves our wellbeing.

Recognizing these barriers represents the first step toward restoring our intuitive flow. By understanding how modern life interferes with our natural intuitive capabilities, we can begin to make conscious choices that protect and nurture this vital inner resource. Creating regular periods of digital detox, spending time in nature, practicing mindfulness, and prioritizing adequate rest can help rebuild our intuitive connections despite these contemporary challenges.

The Paradox of Structured Spontaneity

Structured spontaneity represents one of the most intriguing paradoxes in human experience, particularly when it comes to developing and trusting our intuitive abilities. Like a jazz musician who masters scales before improvising freely, we often find that structure provides the foundation for our most spontaneous and intuitive moments.

The human mind naturally seeks patterns and organization, yet our most creative and intuitive insights often emerge from moments of apparent chaos. This seeming contradiction reveals a deeper truth about how intuition operates within the framework of our lives. When we create intentional structures, we actually free our minds to explore spontaneous possibilities more fully.

Consider the practice of meditation, where the structured discipline of sitting quietly at the same time each day creates space for spontaneous insights to arise. The regularity of the practice itself serves as a container that allows the mind to release its usual controlling patterns. Paradoxically, it's through this voluntary constraint that we access greater freedom of thought and perception.

Artists and creators have long understood this principle. A painter works within the confined space of a canvas, using specific materials and techniques, yet these very limitations often spark the most innovative expressions. The structure of their craft provides the security needed for spontaneous creativity to flourish.

In professional settings, we see this paradox at work when well-designed systems and protocols actually enable faster, more intuitive decision-making. When basic procedures are clearly established, professionals can focus their intuitive capabilities on more complex aspects of their work rather than getting bogged down in routine decisions.

The body itself demonstrates this principle through the heart's rhythmic beating – a highly structured process that nonetheless responds spontaneously to changing conditions. This biological wisdom suggests that structure and spontaneity are not opponents but partners in creating optimal function.

Regular daily routines, rather than limiting spontaneity, often enhance our ability to act intuitively when unexpected situations arise. By handling routine matters efficiently within a structured framework, we preserve mental and emotional energy for spontaneous responses when they're truly needed.

Athletes exemplify structured spontaneity through their training regimens. The countless hours of structured practice allow them to respond instantaneously and creatively during competition. Their practiced moves become so deeply embedded that spontaneous adaptations flow naturally in the heat of the moment.

Writers who maintain consistent writing schedules often find that their most inspired passages emerge within these structured time blocks. The commitment to showing up regularly at the desk creates the conditions for spontaneous creative flow, demonstrating how discipline can nurture rather than inhibit intuitive expression.

In relationships, having clear boundaries and agreements actually creates more space for genuine spontaneity and emotional authenticity. When basic expectations are understood, people feel secure enough to express themselves more freely and respond more intuitively to each other's needs.

The practice of improvised music offers perhaps the clearest example of this paradox. Musicians spend years mastering scales, chord progressions, and rhythmic patterns – all highly structured elements. Yet this technical foundation enables them to improvise freely, creating new combinations and expressions in the moment.

Nature itself embodies structured spontaneity through the interplay of physical laws and chaotic systems. Snowflakes form according to rigid molecular principles, yet each one manifests uniquely. This natural pattern suggests that structure and spontaneity are complementary forces rather than opposing ones.

Learning to work with this paradox requires understanding that structure need not mean rigidity. Effective structures should be flexible enough to accommodate the unexpected while providing sufficient stability to support growth and exploration. Like a trellis supporting a climbing plant, good structure enables natural development rather than constraining it.

The key lies in creating structures that serve rather than dominate our intuitive processes. This might mean establishing regular practices for reflection or creativity while remaining open to modifying these practices when intuition suggests a different approach. The structure should function as a starting point rather than a limitation.

Time management offers another arena where this paradox plays out. By structuring certain aspects of our schedule, we create pockets of time where spontaneity can flourish. Rather than leaving everything to chance, thoughtful planning actually increases opportunities for intuitive exploration.

Understanding and working with the paradox of structured spontaneity allows us to develop more effective approaches to cultivating intuition. By acknowledging that structure and spontaneity can support rather than oppose each other, we can design practices that honor both our need for stability and our capacity for spontaneous insight.

The art lies in finding the right balance – creating enough structure to provide security and efficiency while maintaining sufficient flexibility to allow for intuitive adaptation and creative response. This balance varies for each individual and may shift across different contexts and life phases.

Chapter 2: The Control Systems That Shape Our Decisions

Social Programming and Intuitive Suppression

Social programming begins in our earliest years, systematically eroding our natural intuitive abilities through a complex web of cultural conditioning, educational practices, and societal expectations. From the moment we enter the formal education system, we're taught to prioritize external validation over internal knowing, creating deep-seated patterns that suppress our intuitive wisdom.

The process starts subtly in childhood, when natural intuitive responses are often dismissed or corrected by well-meaning adults. A child who instinctively withdraws from certain situations or individuals might be labeled as shy or antisocial, rather than having their intuitive responses respected and understood. This early programming teaches children to doubt their inner guidance system.

Educational institutions further reinforce this suppression by emphasizing standardized testing and logical reasoning while marginalizing intuitive learning styles. Students quickly learn that success comes from memorizing accepted answers rather than exploring their own inner knowing. This systematic devaluation of intuitive intelligence creates a persistent disconnect between what we feel internally and what we're taught to express externally.

Media and advertising contribute significantly to intuitive suppression by constantly bombarding us with messages about how we should think, feel, and behave. These external influences create a thick layer of noise that drowns out the subtle signals of intuition, replacing authentic inner guidance with manufactured desires and artificial needs.

Professional environments often complete the programming by rewarding conformity and punishing deviation from established norms. Workers learn to suppress their intuitive warnings about toxic situations or unsound decisions, fearing the professional consequences of challenging authority or questioning conventional wisdom.

Social media platforms intensify this programming through sophisticated algorithms that shape our perceptions and beliefs. The constant stream of curated content creates an artificial reality that further distances us from our intuitive understanding of the world. We begin to see ourselves and others through the lens of likes, shares, and carefully constructed online personas.

Religious and cultural institutions frequently contribute to intuitive suppression by establishing rigid frameworks for understanding reality. While these institutions may have originated from genuine intuitive insights, they often evolve into systems that discourage direct personal experience in favor of prescribed beliefs and behaviors.

Gender-based programming particularly impacts intuitive expression, with many societies still conditioning people to suppress or ignore their intuitive feelings based on gender expectations. Men are often taught to dismiss their emotional intuition as weakness, while women may be criticized for trusting their intuitive judgment in professional settings.

The medical establishment sometimes reinforces intuitive suppression by dismissing bodily intuition and subjective experience in favor of standardized protocols. Patients learn to doubt their internal sensing of what their bodies need, deferring instead to external authority figures and diagnostic procedures.

Consumer culture thrives on suppressing intuitive satisfaction, creating artificial desires that override our natural sense of enough. Marketing techniques specifically target and manipulate our emotional responses, making it increasingly difficult to distinguish between genuine intuitive needs and programmed wants.

Political systems maintain their power partly through the suppression of collective intuitive wisdom. By creating artificial divisions and controlling narratives, these systems prevent people from trusting their intuitive understanding of social issues and human relationships.

Language itself serves as a powerful tool for intuitive suppression, with many modern languages lacking adequate vocabulary to describe intuitive experiences. This linguistic limitation makes it difficult to validate and communicate intuitive insights, further marginalizing their importance in daily life.

The contemporary emphasis on constant productivity leaves little room for the quiet reflection necessary for intuitive processing. We're programmed to view any non-productive time as wasted time, creating a perpetual state of activity that blocks intuitive awareness.

Financial systems generate persistent anxiety that interferes with intuitive clarity, programming us to prioritize immediate security over deeper intuitive guidance about our life path and choices. The fear of economic instability often overrides intuitive wisdom about career changes or life transitions.

Entertainment media programs passive consumption over active intuitive engagement, training us to seek external stimulation rather than internal wisdom. The constant availability of entertainment options makes it increasingly difficult to sit with the discomfort that often precedes intuitive breakthrough.

Breaking free from this programming requires conscious effort and sustained practice. It involves recognizing these conditioning patterns and actively creating space for intuitive wisdom to re-emerge. This might mean establishing regular periods of silence, practicing mindful awareness, or seeking out communities that value intuitive knowledge.

The journey of reclaiming our intuitive capabilities often begins with acknowledging how deeply this social programming has affected us. By understanding these mechanisms of suppression, we can begin to dismantle their influence and rebuild trust in our inner guidance system.

Digital Age Interference

Electromagnetic waves from countless devices flood our modern environment, creating an invisible web of interference that profoundly impacts our intuitive capabilities. This digital soup we constantly swim in has transformed not only how we communicate and work but also how our bodies and minds process subtle information.

The average person now spends over seven hours daily interacting with screens, each moment of digital engagement creating a barrier between ourselves and our natural intuitive processes. These devices emit specific frequencies that can disrupt our body's natural electromagnetic field, potentially interfering with the subtle energetic mechanisms through which intuition operates.

Sleep patterns suffer significantly from blue light exposure, affecting the very foundation of our intuitive capacity. The pineal gland, often associated with intuitive perception, becomes particularly disrupted by nighttime screen use. Research indicates that evening exposure to digital devices can suppress melatonin production by up to 40%, directly impacting our ability to enter the deeper states of consciousness where intuition often flourishes.

Push notifications create persistent interruptions that fragment our attention span. Each ping triggers a dopamine response, training our brains to seek constant external stimulation rather than tuning into our inner guidance. This pavlovian conditioning makes it increasingly difficult to maintain the sustained focus necessary for intuitive insights to emerge.

Social media platforms specifically design their interfaces to bypass our natural decision-making processes, creating addictive patterns that override intuitive wisdom. The endless scroll feature exploits our natural curiosity while simultaneously exhausting our mental resources, leaving little energy for deeper intuitive processing.

Virtual relationships, while valuable in their own right, often lack the energetic component that supports intuitive understanding between people. The subtle cues we naturally pick up in face-to-face interactions become lost in digital translation, weakening our ability to trust and develop our interpersonal intuition.

The constant availability of information has created a dependency on external validation, reducing our trust in personal intuitive knowledge. Rather than sitting with uncertainty and allowing intuitive insights to emerge, we immediately reach for our devices to find answers, gradually atrophying our natural problem-solving abilities.

Digital multitasking has become normalized, despite research showing it reduces cognitive performance and intuitive capacity. When we rapidly switch between tasks and devices, we create neural patterns that favor shallow processing over the deeper states where intuition operates most effectively.

Location-based services and GPS technology, while convenient, have diminished our natural spatial awareness and navigational intuition. The constant reliance on digital guidance systems weakens our innate ability to sense direction and location, skills that once formed a crucial part of human intuitive capacity.

Online shopping algorithms predict and influence our choices, gradually replacing genuine intuitive desire with artificially generated wants. These sophisticated systems study our behavior patterns and exploit psychological vulnerabilities, making it increasingly difficult to distinguish between authentic intuitive preferences and programmed responses.

Digital communication platforms often strip away the nuanced emotional content of human interaction, creating a flattened experience that fails to engage our full range of intuitive perception. Emoji and reaction buttons serve as poor substitutes for the rich emotional landscape that supports intuitive understanding.

Cloud storage and digital memory have externalized our knowledge base, potentially weakening our natural capacity for intuitive recall and pattern recognition. When we constantly defer to stored digital information, we may be reducing our brain's ability to make the spontaneous connections that often characterize intuitive insights.

The rise of digital entertainment has created unprecedented competition for our attention, making it increasingly difficult to achieve the quiet mental states conducive to intuitive processing. Streaming services, gaming platforms, and social media compete aggressively for our limited attention resources.

Remote work environments, while offering many benefits, can create a disconnection from the physical and energetic cues that often inform workplace intuition. The ability to read a room or sense the underlying dynamics of a situation becomes compromised in virtual settings.

Digital security concerns generate a background level of anxiety that can interfere with intuitive flow. The constant threat of data breaches, identity theft, and online surveillance creates a subtle but persistent stress that may inhibit our ability to access deeper intuitive wisdom.

Yet within this challenging landscape, opportunities exist to maintain and strengthen our intuitive capabilities. Creating dedicated device-free periods, establishing digital boundaries, and consciously engaging with the physical world can help preserve our intuitive functions. Regular breaks from screen time, combined with practices that enhance body awareness and natural rhythms, can help counteract digital interference.

Understanding these digital age challenges allows us to make more conscious choices about our technology use. By recognizing how digital interference affects our intuitive capabilities, we can develop strategies to protect and nurture this essential aspect of human consciousness while still benefiting from technological advancement.

Data-Driven Decision Making vs. Intuitive Wisdom

The tension between analytical data and intuitive wisdom creates one of the most significant challenges in modern decision-making. While data provides concrete metrics and measurable outcomes, intuitive wisdom offers deeper insights that often transcend what numbers alone can reveal. This dynamic interplay deserves careful examination as we navigate increasingly complex choices in both personal and professional spheres.

Data-driven approaches have revolutionized how organizations and individuals make decisions, offering unprecedented access to information and statistical analysis. Spreadsheets, algorithms, and metrics provide a sense of security and objectivity that appeals to our rational minds. However, this reliance on pure data often overlooks crucial nuances that intuitive wisdom naturally encompasses.

Consider the story of Sarah, a successful investment manager who faced a critical decision about a seemingly promising merger. While all the financial data indicated a profitable venture, her gut feeling signaled warning signs. Despite pressure from colleagues and impressive projections, she trusted her intuition and declined the deal. Months later, hidden liabilities emerged that would have devastated the investment – factors her intuitive wisdom had somehow sensed beyond the numbers.

Research in neuroscience reveals that our brains process vastly more information than we consciously analyze. The intuitive mind can integrate thousands of subtle variables simultaneously, whereas data-driven analysis typically focuses on a limited set of measurable factors. This broader processing capacity explains why intuitive insights sometimes prove more accurate than detailed statistical analysis.

Corporate environments often dismiss intuitive wisdom in favor of data-driven metrics, creating a dangerous imbalance. While key performance indicators and return on investment calculations provide valuable insights, they can miss crucial qualitative factors like team dynamics, cultural fit, or long-term sustainability. The most effective leaders learn to balance both approaches, using data to inform their decisions while remaining attuned to intuitive signals.

Historical examples repeatedly demonstrate the limitations of pure data-driven decision-making. The 2008 financial crisis emerged partly because complex mathematical models failed to account for human behavior and market psychology – factors that many intuitive observers had flagged as concerning. Similarly, successful entrepreneurs often credit key decisions to intuitive feelings that defied contemporary market data.

The healthcare sector illustrates this dynamic particularly well. While medical decisions increasingly rely on evidence-based protocols, experienced physicians often detect subtle patterns and potential issues through intuitive observation that standard tests might miss. The most effective healthcare practitioners combine rigorous data analysis with finely-tuned intuitive awareness.

Personal relationships represent another arena where data-driven approaches fall short. While personality assessments and compatibility metrics provide interesting insights, genuine connection and understanding often emerge from intuitive awareness. The success of a relationship rarely correlates with how well it matches on paper.

Educational systems heavily favor data-driven assessment, potentially undermining students' natural intuitive capabilities. Standardized testing and quantitative evaluations, while useful for certain measurements, often fail to capture deeper understanding and creative potential. This imbalance can produce graduates who excel at analysis but struggle with intuitive problem-solving.

The creative arts demonstrate the essential role of intuitive wisdom. While data can inform aspects of artistic creation, genuine innovation and emotional resonance spring from intuitive sources. Even in commercial creative endeavors, the most successful works often arise from choices that transcend market research and demographic data.

Environmental decisions particularly benefit from combining both approaches. While scientific data provides crucial information about ecological systems, intuitive wisdom often guides sustainable practices and harmonious relationships with nature. Indigenous cultures have long demonstrated how intuitive understanding of natural systems can surpass purely analytical approaches.

Modern technology offers opportunities to bridge this divide. Some innovative organizations now develop systems that incorporate both data analytics and intuitive insights, recognizing that the strongest decisions emerge from their integration. These hybrid approaches show promising results in fields ranging from urban planning to product development.

The key lies not in choosing between data and intuition but in understanding their complementary nature. Data provides valuable framework and verification, while intuitive wisdom offers deeper insight and holistic understanding. Learning to weave these approaches together creates more robust decision-making processes.

Developing this balanced approach requires conscious practice. It involves cultivating awareness of both analytical and intuitive inputs, recognizing their respective strengths and limitations. Regular reflection on past decisions can help identify patterns where either data or intuition proved particularly valuable.

The future of decision-making likely lies in approaches that honor both data-driven analysis and intuitive wisdom. As we face increasingly complex challenges, the ability to integrate these complementary ways of knowing becomes ever more crucial. Success depends on developing frameworks that allow both forms of intelligence to inform our choices.

This integration represents not just a practical necessity but an opportunity for more comprehensive understanding. By embracing both data-driven and intuitive approaches, we access a fuller spectrum of human intelligence and decision-making capability.

Chapter 3: Mapping the Intuition Protocol

Core Components of Intuitive Processing

Intuitive processing operates through distinct yet interconnected components that form the foundation of our inner guidance system. Understanding these core elements helps unlock the full potential of our intuitive capabilities and allows us to develop them more effectively.

The body's sensory system serves as the primary gateway for intuitive information. Beyond the five conventional senses, our bodies possess subtle receptors that process information below the threshold of conscious awareness. These receptors respond to electromagnetic fields, subtle energy variations, and minute changes in our environment that our rational minds might overlook.

Emotional intelligence forms another crucial component, acting as an interpreter for intuitive signals. Our emotional responses often contain valuable information about situations and people, providing instant feedback before logical analysis can begin. These emotional cues arise from complex neural networks throughout the body, particularly in the heart and gut regions, which contain sophisticated processing centers often referred to as the "second and third brains."

Pattern recognition capabilities represent a fundamental aspect of intuitive processing. Our brains constantly scan for meaningful connections and relationships, drawing upon vast repositories of stored experiences. This unconscious pattern matching occurs at speeds far exceeding conscious thought, allowing us to make rapid assessments and predictions based on subtle environmental cues.

The enteric nervous system, located in our digestive tract, plays a vital role in intuitive processing. This complex network of neurons processes information independently of our conscious mind, generating what we often call "gut feelings." Research indicates that this system communicates directly with our brain, influencing decision-making and emotional responses.

Mirror neurons contribute significantly to our intuitive understanding of others. These specialized brain cells activate both when we perform an action and when we observe others performing similar actions, creating an internal simulation that helps us understand intentions and emotions. This mechanism underlies our ability to empathize and read social situations intuitively.

Time perception represents another key component of intuitive processing. Our intuitive mind can process information from past, present, and potential future scenarios simultaneously, creating what some researchers call "time-collapsed" awareness. This ability allows us to sense potential outcomes and make split-second decisions based on complex temporal patterns.

The heart's electromagnetic field serves as a powerful intuitive antenna. Extending several feet beyond our bodies, this field interacts with others' energy fields and environmental information. The heart's rhythm patterns change in response to emotional and intuitive signals, often before conscious awareness of a situation develops.

Cellular memory plays a crucial role in intuitive processing. Every cell in our body stores information and responds to environmental signals, creating a distributed intelligence network that contributes to our intuitive awareness. This cellular wisdom accumulates throughout our lives, enriching our intuitive capabilities with each experience.

The right hemisphere of the brain specializes in holistic processing, handling information in patterns and wholes rather than sequential parts. This hemispheric function proves essential for intuitive insights, allowing us to grasp complex situations instantly without step-by-step analysis.

Biorhythms and natural cycles influence our intuitive processing capacity. Our bodies maintain numerous internal rhythms that align with natural cycles, affecting our receptivity to intuitive information. Understanding and working with these rhythms can enhance our intuitive abilities.

The pineal gland, often called the "third eye," functions as a critical component in intuitive processing. This small endocrine gland responds to light and electromagnetic fields, potentially serving as a biological antenna for subtle information. Its production of melatonin and other compounds influences our consciousness and receptivity to intuitive insights.

Quantum field interactions may underlie many aspects of intuitive processing. Emerging research suggests that our bodies can detect and respond to quantum-level information, potentially explaining how intuitive insights can transcend ordinary space-time limitations.

The vagus nerve, connecting our brain with major organs, acts as a primary channel for intuitive information. This extensive nerve network facilitates rapid communication between our gut instincts, heart intelligence, and cognitive processes, integrating various forms of intuitive input.

Memory consolidation during sleep plays a vital role in developing intuitive capabilities. During sleep, our brains process and integrate experiences, strengthening the neural networks that support intuitive pattern recognition and decision-making.

The autonomic nervous system continuously monitors our environment and internal state, providing crucial background information for intuitive processing. This system responds to subtle threats and opportunities before conscious awareness, preparing our bodies for appropriate action.

Understanding these core components allows us to develop practices that enhance their function and integration. Regular meditation, body awareness exercises, and attention to emotional signals can strengthen these natural intuitive processing systems. Additionally, reducing interference from stress and digital distraction helps maintain the sensitivity of these delicate mechanisms.

By recognizing and nurturing these fundamental aspects of intuitive processing, we can develop a more refined and reliable intuitive guidance system. This enhanced awareness leads to better decision-making, deeper understanding, and more authentic living aligned with our inner wisdom.

Breaking Through Rational Resistance

Rational resistance forms a formidable barrier between us and our intuitive wisdom, manifesting as an internal struggle that can paralyze decision-making and personal growth. Breaking through this resistance requires understanding its roots and developing practical strategies to overcome it.

The story of Maria, a talented architect, illustrates this common struggle. Despite her strong intuitive pull toward sustainable design, she repeatedly suppressed these inclinations in favor of conventional approaches backed by traditional market data. Her rational mind constructed elaborate arguments against following her inner guidance, citing risk factors and industry standards. Only after a particularly unsatisfying project did she recognize how this resistance had limited her creative potential and professional fulfillment.

Our educational and professional systems heavily reinforce rational resistance through their emphasis on measurable outcomes and logical analysis. From early schooling through career advancement, we learn to distrust subtle feelings and internal knowing in favor of external validation and concrete evidence. This conditioning creates deep-seated patterns that automatically reject intuitive insights that don't align with conventional reasoning.

Physical manifestations often accompany rational resistance. Tension headaches, tight shoulders, and digestive issues frequently signal the body's response to suppressing intuitive wisdom. These physical symptoms create a feedback loop, further reinforcing the dominance of rational thinking over intuitive knowing. Learning to recognize and release these bodily patterns becomes essential in dismantling resistance.

Fear plays a central role in maintaining rational barriers. The fear of making mistakes, appearing irrational, or facing judgment from others keeps many people firmly anchored in logical thinking patterns. This fear-based approach creates a self-reinforcing cycle where intuitive signals become increasingly difficult to trust or even recognize.

Breaking through requires understanding that rational thought and intuition serve complementary purposes. Logic excels at analyzing known factors and past patterns, while intuition accesses deeper wisdom and future possibilities. Neither approach alone provides complete understanding, and both deserve respect and integration.

Small daily practices help weaken rational resistance effectively. Starting with low-stakes decisions allows safe exploration of intuitive guidance without triggering strong defensive reactions. For instance, practicing intuitive eating by trusting body signals about hunger and fullness can build confidence in inner knowing.

Mindfulness practices prove particularly powerful in dissolving rational resistance. Regular meditation creates space between thoughts, allowing intuitive insights to surface more easily. Even five minutes of quiet reflection each day can begin to shift the balance between analytical and intuitive processing.

Body-based practices offer another pathway through resistance. Movement activities like dance, yoga, or walking in nature engage non-verbal intelligence and create new neural pathways that support intuitive processing. These practices help bypass the analytical mind's tendency to override subtle internal signals.

Journaling about intuitive experiences helps document the accuracy of inner guidance, providing evidence that can satisfy the rational mind's need for verification. Recording instances where intuition proved correct builds trust in this natural capacity for knowing.

Working with dreams offers a direct route around rational resistance. Dreams naturally bypass logical filters, providing access to intuitive wisdom through symbols and metaphors. Keeping a dream journal and reflecting on dream messages strengthens trust in non-rational sources of knowledge.

Support from others who value intuitive wisdom can help overcome rational resistance. Sharing experiences with trusted friends or joining groups that honor inner knowing provides validation and encouragement for developing these capacities. This social support helps counter the dominant cultural emphasis on pure logic.

Nature immersion naturally weakens rational resistance by engaging our innate sensing abilities. Time spent in natural settings helps restore balance between analytical and intuitive processing. The natural world operates through intricate patterns that our intuitive mind readily grasps.

Understanding that rational resistance serves a protective function allows us to approach it with compassion rather than frustration. This resistance developed for valid reasons but now requires gentle reorganization to allow fuller access to our complete range of knowing.

Professional situations often trigger strong rational resistance due to expectations of evidence-based decision-making. Developing strategies to incorporate intuitive insights while meeting organizational requirements becomes crucial. This might involve gathering supporting data after receiving intuitive guidance or framing intuitive insights in terms acceptable to stakeholders.

The process of breaking through rational resistance opens doorways to enhanced perception and understanding. As the barrier softens, integration between logical and intuitive capabilities creates more comprehensive wisdom and better decision-making abilities. This integration leads to more satisfying personal and professional choices aligned with deeper knowing.

The Role of Emotional Intelligence

Emotional intelligence forms the cornerstone of intuitive development, serving as a bridge between conscious awareness and deeper understanding. This sophisticated capacity enables us to recognize, interpret, and respond to the subtle emotional signals that guide intuitive insights.

Sarah, a seasoned therapist, demonstrates the power of emotional intelligence in professional settings. During a routine session, she noticed a slight shift in her client's tone when discussing family relationships. While the client's words remained positive, Sarah's emotional attunement detected underlying distress, leading to a breakthrough conversation about unresolved grief. This emotional awareness allowed her to guide the session more effectively than logical analysis alone would have permitted.

The foundation of emotional intelligence rests on self-awareness, the ability to recognize and understand our own emotional states. This awareness extends beyond simple recognition of primary emotions like happiness or anger, encompassing subtle variations and complex emotional blends. These nuanced emotional signals often carry important intuitive information about situations or relationships.

Body-emotion connections play a crucial role in developing emotional intelligence. Physical sensations frequently accompany emotional states, creating a complex feedback system that informs intuitive understanding. Learning to Interpret these bodily signals enhances our ability to access emotional wisdom quickly and accurately.

Empathic capacity grows naturally with increased emotional intelligence. The ability to sense and understand others' emotional states provides valuable information about interpersonal dynamics and potential outcomes. This skill operates below conscious awareness, drawing on subtle cues in facial expressions, body language, and energetic patterns.

Emotional regulation skills support intuitive development by maintaining clear channels for receiving intuitive information. When emotions become overwhelming or suppressed, they can distort intuitive signals. Balanced emotional states allow for more accurate interpretation of intuitive insights.

The heart's electromagnetic field plays a significant role in emotional intelligence. Research indicates that this field extends several feet beyond the body and responds to emotional states. This sensitivity allows us to detect emotional information from others before conscious awareness occurs.

Cultural conditioning often interferes with emotional intelligence development. Many societies value rational thought over emotional wisdom, leading to disconnection from this vital source of information. Recognizing and challenging these cultural barriers helps restore natural emotional intelligence.

Professional environments particularly benefit from developed emotional intelligence. Leaders who combine emotional awareness with technical expertise make more effective decisions and build stronger teams. Their intuitive understanding of group dynamics and individual needs creates more productive and harmonious workplaces.

Emotional intelligence enhances personal relationships through improved communication and understanding. The ability to sense underlying emotional currents helps navigate complex interpersonal situations and maintain deeper connections. This capacity often prevents conflicts before they escalate.

Memory processing involves emotional intelligence in significant ways. Emotional context influences how we store and retrieve information, affecting our ability to learn from experience. This emotional memory system contributes to intuitive pattern recognition and quick assessment of situations.

Stress management improves through developed emotional intelligence. The ability to recognize early signs of stress and respond appropriately prevents emotional overload. This maintenance of emotional balance supports clearer intuitive perception.

Decision-making benefits from emotional intelligence through integration of feeling-based wisdom with logical analysis. Research shows that people with damaged emotional processing centers struggle to make effective decisions despite intact rational capabilities. This demonstrates the essential role of emotional intelligence in sound judgment.

Creative expression flows more freely with developed emotional intelligence. Access to subtle emotional states enhances artistic sensitivity and innovation. This emotional awareness allows for more authentic and impactful creative work.

Children naturally display high emotional intelligence before cultural conditioning diminishes this capacity. Observing young children's emotional wisdom reminds us of our innate abilities and the importance of maintaining this natural gift throughout life.

Physical health responds to emotional intelligence through improved stress management and better lifestyle choices. The ability to recognize and respond to emotional needs helps maintain overall wellbeing. This mind-body connection highlights the practical benefits of developed emotional intelligence.

Relationship patterns become clearer through emotional intelligence. Recognition of emotional dynamics helps identify healthy and unhealthy relationships early. This awareness guides better partner choices and more satisfying connections.

Daily practices strengthen emotional intelligence through regular attention to emotional states. Simple check-ins throughout the day build awareness and responsiveness to emotional signals. This consistent practice develops stronger intuitive capabilities over time.

The integration of emotional intelligence with other aspects of personal development creates a more complete and effective approach to life. This holistic development supports better decision-making, stronger relationships, and more authentic living aligned with inner wisdom.

Physical Signals and Bodily Wisdom

Our bodies communicate through an intricate language of sensations, tensions, and subtle energetic shifts that often precede conscious awareness. This physical intelligence operates continuously, offering valuable guidance that many of us have learned to override or ignore in our mentally-oriented culture.

David, an experienced trader, discovered the importance of bodily wisdom after a costly market decision. Despite feeling a distinct tightness in his stomach before making a significant investment, he dismissed this physical warning signal in favor of promising market analytics. The subsequent loss taught him to respect these bodily cues, leading to more balanced and successful trading decisions.

The stomach serves as a particularly sensitive indicator of intuitive information. Often called our "second brain," the enteric nervous system contains millions of neurons that process information independently from our conscious mind. That "gut feeling" represents genuine neural activity responding to subtle environmental and interpersonal cues.

Heart rhythms change in response to intuitive information before the conscious mind registers danger or opportunity. Research has shown that the heart responds to future events several seconds before they occur, demonstrating the body's capacity for precognitive awareness. This cardiac intelligence offers reliable guidance when we learn to attend to its signals.

Muscle tension patterns often reflect blocked intuitive messages. The shoulders, neck, and jaw commonly hold stress when we resist inner knowing. Regular body scanning helps identify these areas of resistance, allowing release of physical barriers to intuitive flow. Simple awareness often initiates natural unwinding of these protective patterns.

Breathing patterns shift in response to intuitive information. Shallow breathing typically indicates resistance to intuitive messages, while deep, relaxed breathing supports clearer reception. Conscious breath work helps restore natural respiratory rhythms and enhances bodily wisdom access.

The hands contain sophisticated sensing capabilities beyond ordinary touch. Subtle temperature changes, tingling sensations, or pressure awareness in the palms often signal intuitive information. Energy healers and bodyworkers regularly utilize this hand sensitivity in their practice.

Spinal alignment influences intuitive reception. The vertebral column serves as an antenna for subtle information, with misalignments potentially blocking clear transmission. Regular movement practices help maintain optimal spinal function and enhance intuitive flow.

Sleep patterns provide important intuitive information through dreams and body signals. Waking at specific times, experiencing unusual physical sensations, or receiving vivid dreams often carry meaningful messages. Recording these patterns reveals valuable insights about health and life direction.

Physical symptoms frequently represent unacknowledged intuitive messages. Headaches, digestive issues, or recurring pain may indicate resistance to inner guidance. Approaching these symptoms with curious attention often reveals their deeper meaning and resolution path.

Energy levels fluctuate in response to environments and situations that affect our wellbeing. Sudden fatigue in specific locations or with certain people often signals energetic incompatibility. Learning to honor these energy shifts supports better boundary setting and self-care.

Movement practices enhance bodily wisdom connection. Dance, yoga, martial arts, or spontaneous motion helps bypass mental resistance and access direct physical knowing. These activities develop greater trust in body intelligence and improve intuitive reception.

Temperature sensitivity often accompanies intuitive information. Unexpected cold spots, warm sensations, or localized temperature changes may signal energetic presence or important messages. Developing awareness of these thermal shifts enhances intuitive recognition.

Visual signals manifest through physical symptoms like eye strain, blurred vision, or seeing movement in peripheral vision. These optical experiences sometimes precede significant events or carry important warnings. Regular eye relaxation supports clearer intuitive vision.

The immune system responds to intuitive information through subtle changes in health status. Mild symptoms often serve as early warning signals about situations or relationships that may prove harmful. Attending to these physical messages supports better life choices.

Physical attraction or repulsion provides valuable intuitive guidance about people and situations. These bodily responses often prove more reliable than mental analysis in relationship decisions. Learning to trust these instinctive reactions leads to better personal and professional associations.

Voice changes often reflect blocked intuitive messages. Throat tightness, loss of volume, or pitch changes may signal resistance to speaking truth or acting on inner knowing. Working with sound and vibration helps clear these vocal restrictions.

Posture automatically adjusts to reflect our relationship with truth and power. Slouching, throat covering, or protective stances often indicate compromise of authentic expression. Conscious posture awareness helps identify situations requiring attention to personal truth.

Developing trust in bodily wisdom requires regular practice and validation through experience. Starting with small decisions and noting physical signals helps build confidence in this natural guidance system. Over time, this physical intelligence becomes a reliable partner in navigating life's challenges and opportunities.

Integrating Multiple Information Streams

The symphony of information constantly flowing through our awareness requires skillful integration to extract meaningful guidance. Like a master conductor coordinating various instrumental sections, we must learn to harmonize different streams of information to create a coherent understanding of our experiences.

Rachel, a successful emergency room physician, exemplifies this integration process in action. During a particularly challenging case, she simultaneously processed the patient's vital signs, subtle body language, team dynamics, and her own gut feelings. This integrated awareness led her to investigate beyond standard protocols, ultimately discovering a rare condition that might have been missed through conventional analysis alone.

Our sensory systems provide the foundation for information integration. Visual, auditory, kinesthetic, olfactory, and gustatory inputs combine with subtle energetic perceptions to create a complete picture of any situation. Learning to consciously attend to all these channels enhances our ability to receive and interpret complex information patterns.

The brain's natural filtering system typically reduces incoming data to manageable levels, sometimes excluding vital intuitive information. Developing awareness of this filtering process allows us to adjust our receptivity and capture previously ignored signals. Regular meditation practice helps expand this perceptual bandwidth.

Time-based information arrives through multiple streams, including memories, present moment awareness, and future possibilities. Integrating these temporal perspectives creates richer understanding and more effective decision-making. Past experiences inform present choices while intuitive future sensing guides long-term direction.

Emotional data flows continuously, carrying valuable information about relationships and situations. Combining emotional awareness with logical analysis and physical sensations creates more accurate assessments than any single information stream alone. This emotional integration supports better personal and professional choices.

Environmental signals contribute important information through subtle changes in temperature, air pressure, and electromagnetic fields. These ambient conditions affect our physical and psychological states, influencing intuitive reception. Developing sensitivity to environmental factors enhances overall information integration.

Social dynamics generate complex information patterns through verbal and non-verbal communication. Group energy fields, individual relationships, and collective emotions create intricate webs of information requiring sophisticated integration. Understanding these social patterns improves leadership and collaboration.

Dreams provide unique information streams combining symbolic, emotional, and precognitive elements. Integrating dream content with waking experience reveals deeper patterns and potential futures. Regular dream work strengthens overall information processing capabilities.

Physical symptoms carry messages about health, relationships, and life direction. Combining body awareness with emotional understanding and mental analysis creates comprehensive health insights. This integrated approach supports better treatment choices and preventive care.

Creative expression often emerges from successful integration of multiple information streams. Artists, musicians, and writers draw upon diverse inputs to create meaningful works. This creative synthesis demonstrates the power of unified information processing.

Decision-making improves dramatically when multiple information streams inform choices. Combining analytical data with emotional intelligence, physical signals, and intuitive guidance leads to more effective outcomes. This integrated approach prevents common decision-making pitfalls.

Professional expertise develops through integration of technical knowledge with experiential wisdom. Master practitioners in any field combine formal training with subtle pattern recognition and intuitive understanding. This integration produces superior results compared to technical skill alone.

Relationship dynamics become clearer through integrated information processing. Combining verbal and non-verbal cues with emotional awareness and energetic sensitivity reveals authentic connection possibilities. This comprehensive understanding supports better relationship choices.

Learning accelerates when multiple information channels reinforce key concepts. Visual, auditory, and kinesthetic inputs combine with emotional engagement to create lasting understanding. This integrated learning approach develops deeper wisdom and practical skill.

Problem-solving benefits from simultaneous processing of logical, emotional, and intuitive information. Complex challenges often require insights from multiple perspectives for effective resolution. Integration of diverse information streams reveals innovative solutions.

Energy awareness adds another dimension to information processing. Subtle energy fields carry information about health, relationships, and environmental conditions. Including energetic awareness in our integration practice expands understanding and effectiveness.

Communication improves through attention to multiple information channels. Combining verbal content with tone, body language, and energetic presence creates more impactful expression. This integrated communication style enhances personal and professional relationships.

Regular practice strengthens our capacity to process multiple information streams simultaneously. Starting with simple exercises and gradually increasing complexity builds natural integration abilities. This developmental approach prevents overwhelm while expanding capability.

The art of information integration ultimately leads to wisdom - the ability to understand and act appropriately in any situation. This wisdom emerges naturally as we learn to harmonize different streams of knowledge and experience into coherent understanding.

Chapter 4: Developing the Protocol

Baseline Assessment Methods

Establishing accurate baselines provides essential reference points for measuring intuitive development and validating personal experiences. Much like a scientist needs control conditions for experiments, practitioners require clear standards to evaluate their progress and verify intuitive signals.

Marina, a business consultant, discovered the power of baseline assessment when developing her intuitive skills. She began by documenting her normal stress levels, energy patterns, and physical sensations during routine activities. This careful observation allowed her to quickly identify subtle shifts that signaled important information during client meetings, ultimately enhancing her consulting effectiveness.

Physical baseline measurements include regular body temperature, heart rate, and breathing patterns under various conditions. Tracking these vital signs helps distinguish between normal fluctuations and intuitive signals. Many practitioners maintain simple journals recording these measurements at different times of day.

Emotional baselines establish typical mood patterns and reaction tendencies. Understanding personal emotional rhythms helps identify unusual responses that may carry intuitive information. Regular emotional check-ins throughout the day build this fundamental awareness.

Energy levels naturally fluctuate according to daily and seasonal cycles. Documenting these patterns creates reference points for recognizing significant deviations. Unusual energy shifts often precede important events or signal needed adjustments in activities.

Sleep patterns provide valuable baseline information about natural rhythms and restoration needs. Recording sleep quality, duration, and dream frequency establishes normal parameters. Departures from these patterns frequently carry meaningful messages about health and life direction.

Environmental sensitivity varies among individuals and circumstances. Establishing personal thresholds for noise, light, and social stimulation helps identify optimal conditions for intuitive reception. This awareness supports better boundary setting and environment selection.

Thought patterns reveal habitual mental tendencies and beliefs. Observing these patterns helps distinguish between conditioned responses and genuine intuitive insights. Regular meditation practice enhances this mental baseline awareness.

Decision-making typically follows personal patterns in different situations. Understanding these patterns helps identify when intuitive guidance suggests alternative approaches. Tracking decision outcomes validates the value of following intuitive signals.

Relationship dynamics demonstrate consistent patterns in different contexts. Establishing baseline awareness of these patterns helps recognize significant variations that merit attention. This understanding supports better relationship choices and communication.

Professional performance shows natural rhythms and capabilities. Documenting typical work patterns helps identify enhanced functioning through intuitive guidance. This baseline awareness supports career development and time management.

Creative expression follows individual patterns of inspiration and implementation. Understanding these patterns helps distinguish between forced effort and genuine creative flow. Regular creative practice builds this baseline awareness.

Physical space arrangements carry specific energy patterns that affect intuitive reception. Documenting these environmental influences establishes optimal conditions for practice and development. Simple space adjustments often enhance intuitive clarity.

Time perception varies under different conditions and activities. Establishing typical time-sense patterns helps identify altered states that may carry intuitive information. This awareness supports better scheduling and activity planning.

Communication styles show consistent patterns in various situations. Understanding personal communication baselines helps identify when intuitive guidance suggests different approaches. This awareness enhances professional and personal interactions.

Learning patterns reveal individual strengths and challenges. Documenting these patterns helps optimize skill development and knowledge integration. Regular self-assessment builds this educational baseline awareness.

Social energy requirements vary among individuals and circumstances. Establishing personal thresholds for interaction helps maintain optimal conditions for intuitive reception. This awareness supports better social choices and energy management.

Problem-solving approaches typically follow individual patterns. Understanding these patterns helps recognize when intuitive guidance offers novel solutions. Regular practice problems build this baseline awareness.

Validation methods require consistent application of baseline measurements. Combining objective data with subjective experience creates reliable assessment standards. This systematic approach builds confidence in intuitive development.

Regular review and adjustment of baseline measurements ensures continued accuracy and relevance. Personal patterns evolve through practice and life changes.

Maintaining current baselines supports ongoing intuitive development and practical application.

Intuition Training Frameworks

Success in developing intuitive abilities relies heavily on structured approaches that systematically build awareness and skill. Just as athletes follow training programs to enhance their performance, intuitive development requires organized frameworks that progress from basic awareness to advanced applications.

Sarah, a corporate strategist, transformed her decision-making process through systematic intuitive training. Beginning with simple exercises in sensory awareness, she gradually expanded her practice to include emotional recognition, energy sensing, and integrated pattern recognition. Within six months, her enhanced intuitive capabilities led to breakthrough insights that significantly improved her company's market position.

Foundation training starts with sensory refinement exercises that sharpen basic perception. Practitioners spend time in nature, focusing on subtle sounds, scents, and visual details often overlooked in daily life. This fundamental practice develops the attention necessary for more sophisticated intuitive work.

Emotional literacy forms a crucial component of intuitive development. Daily emotional check-ins, coupled with detailed journaling, help practitioners distinguish between personal feelings and intuitive information about others. This emotional clarity prevents projection and enhances accuracy.

Energy sensing exercises build upon physical awareness. Simple practices like scanning the energy field around plants or crystals develop subtle perception abilities. These skills gradually extend to reading human energy fields and environmental conditions.

Meditation serves as a core practice in most training frameworks. Regular silent sitting develops mental clarity and reduces interference from random thoughts. Progressive meditation techniques systematically expand awareness while maintaining practical grounding.

Dream work provides valuable training opportunities during sleep states. Keeping detailed dream journals and practicing lucid dreaming techniques develops fluid awareness across different states of consciousness. This expanded perception naturally enhances intuitive capabilities.

Movement practices integrate physical and intuitive awareness. Tai chi, yoga, or free-form dance help practitioners recognize how intuitive information manifests through the body. Regular movement sessions maintain vital mind-body connection.

Validation protocols ensure accurate assessment of intuitive information. Practitioners maintain detailed records of impressions and outcomes, building confidence through documented success. This systematic approach prevents self-deception and supports genuine development.

Time management frameworks balance practice requirements with daily responsibilities. Short, frequent sessions often prove more effective than occasional long practices. Consistent engagement maintains momentum and supports steady progress.

Partnership exercises accelerate development through shared experience and feedback. Working with trained partners provides safe opportunities to test and refine intuitive skills. Regular exchange sessions build confidence and capability.

Environmental training helps practitioners recognize how different settings affect intuitive reception. Systematic exposure to various locations and conditions develops adaptability and resilience. This environmental awareness supports reliable performance across diverse situations.

Professional integration frameworks guide appropriate application of intuitive skills in work settings. Careful attention to ethical considerations and practical limitations ensures responsible implementation. This balanced approach maintains professional credibility.

Relationship dynamics provide rich training opportunities through daily interactions. Structured observation of verbal and non-verbal communication develops pattern recognition skills. These social insights enhance both personal and professional relationships.

Crisis response training prepares practitioners for high-pressure situations requiring quick intuitive guidance. Simulated scenarios build confidence and capability under stress. Regular practice ensures reliable performance when stakes are high.

Advanced frameworks integrate multiple awareness streams into coherent understanding. Practitioners learn to synthesize physical, emotional, mental, and spiritual information. This integrated approach produces comprehensive insights and effective guidance.

Protection protocols ensure energetic safety during intensive practice periods. Regular grounding exercises and energy clearing techniques maintain healthy boundaries. These protective practices prevent burnout and support sustainable development.

Measurement systems track progress through various development stages. Clear benchmarks help practitioners recognize advancement and identify areas needing attention. Regular assessment maintains focused effort and steady improvement.

Cultural integration frameworks help practitioners navigate diverse belief systems and social contexts.

Understanding how intuition manifests across different cultures enhances adaptability and effectiveness. This cultural awareness supports broader application.

The ultimate goal of intuitive training frameworks extends beyond skill development to wisdom cultivation. Through systematic practice, practitioners develop not just ability but mature understanding of appropriate application. This wisdom ensures responsible use of intuitive capabilities in service of greater good.

Protocol Implementation Stages

Mastering intuitive development requires systematic progression through carefully structured implementation stages. Each stage builds upon previous foundations while introducing new challenges and capabilities, creating a comprehensive path toward intuitive mastery.

David, a research scientist, discovered the importance of following proper implementation stages when developing his intuitive abilities. Initially eager to advance quickly, he learned that skipping fundamental stages led to confusion and unreliable results. By returning to basic protocols and progressing systematically, he developed robust intuitive skills that enhanced his scientific work.

The preparation stage establishes essential foundations through basic awareness exercises. Practitioners spend time quieting the mind, observing physical sensations, and noting emotional patterns. This fundamental work typically requires three to six months of regular practice.

During the awareness expansion stage, practitioners develop increased sensitivity to subtle energies and information fields. Simple exercises with plants, crystals, and calm environments build confidence in receiving non-physical information. This stage usually spans four to eight months of dedicated practice.

The validation stage introduces systematic testing of intuitive impressions against verifiable outcomes. Practitioners maintain detailed records of their experiences and results, building evidence-based confidence in their developing abilities. This critical stage often extends six to twelve months.

Integration of intuitive information with analytical thinking characterizes the synthesis stage. Practitioners learn to combine logical assessment with intuitive guidance, creating balanced decision-making processes. This sophisticated integration typically requires eight to fifteen months of practice.

The application stage focuses on implementing intuitive skills in practical situations. Practitioners begin with low-stakes scenarios and gradually progress to more challenging applications. This stage continues indefinitely as capabilities expand.

Throughout the refinement stage, practitioners develop increased precision and reliability in their intuitive reception. Regular calibration exercises and feedback loops support continuous improvement. This ongoing process becomes a lifetime practice.

Protection protocols become increasingly important as sensitivity develops. Practitioners learn energy management techniques, boundary setting, and clearing practices. These protective measures prevent overwhelm and maintain healthy function.

The social integration stage addresses challenges of using intuitive abilities in relationships and professional settings. Practitioners develop appropriate communication strategies and ethical guidelines. This stage requires careful attention to cultural contexts and social norms.

Advanced stages focus on expanding range and depth of intuitive capabilities. Practitioners explore different types of information and various reception methods. This expansion phase builds comprehensive intuitive toolkits for diverse applications.

Crisis response protocols receive special attention during later implementation stages. Practitioners develop reliable performance under pressure through graduated exposure to challenging situations. This preparation ensures dependable function during emergencies.

Documentation becomes increasingly sophisticated as implementation progresses. Practitioners maintain detailed records of experiences, insights, and outcomes. This systematic recording supports both development and validation.

Regular assessment points mark progression through implementation stages. Clear criteria help practitioners recognize advancement and identify areas needing additional work. These checkpoints maintain focused development efforts.

Integration with existing skills and knowledge occurs throughout all stages. Practitioners discover how intuitive capabilities enhance their professional expertise and personal effectiveness. This integration creates practical value from developing abilities.

Environmental factors receive careful consideration during implementation. Practitioners learn to maintain reliable function across different settings and conditions. This adaptability supports consistent performance in varied situations.

Relationship dynamics often shift during implementation stages. Practitioners develop new ways of interacting and sharing information with others. These changes require careful management of personal and professional connections.

Time management becomes increasingly important as practice deepens. Practitioners learn to balance intensive development work with daily responsibilities. This practical scheduling supports sustainable progress.

Advanced protocols introduce sophisticated techniques for specific applications. Practitioners select appropriate methods based on situation and purpose. This targeted approach optimizes effectiveness in different contexts.

The final implementation stage focuses on wisdom development. Practitioners learn to apply their abilities appropriately and ethically. This mature understanding ensures responsible use of intuitive capabilities.

Throughout all stages, maintaining proper sequence and thorough implementation remains essential. While individual progress rates vary, attempting to skip stages typically creates gaps in fundamental capabilities. Patient, systematic progression produces the most reliable results.

Chapter 5: Testing and Validation Methods

Scientific Measurement Tools

Modern scientific tools have revolutionized our ability to measure and validate intuitive phenomena. Through sophisticated equipment and rigorous methodologies, researchers can now quantify previously elusive aspects of intuitive perception and performance.

Rachel, a neuroscience researcher, pioneered the use of advanced brain imaging to study intuitive processing. Her work with functional MRI revealed distinct neural patterns during intuitive decision-making, providing concrete evidence of this natural human capability. The results transformed scientific understanding of intuitive cognition.

Electroencephalography (EEG) equipment offers precise measurement of brain wave patterns during intuitive activities. High-resolution recordings show characteristic shifts in alpha and theta waves when practitioners access intuitive states. These measurements provide objective validation of subjective experiences.

Heart rate variability monitors demonstrate clear correlations between cardiac coherence and intuitive accuracy. Advanced sensors track subtle changes in heart rhythm patterns, revealing how physiological states influence intuitive reception. This data helps practitioners optimize their performance conditions.

Galvanic skin response devices measure subtle changes in electrical conductivity across the skin surface. These measurements often predict intuitive insights seconds before conscious awareness, supporting theories about subconscious information processing.

Environmental sensors detect subtle electromagnetic field variations that may influence intuitive reception. Sophisticated equipment monitors local field strengths and fluctuations, helping identify optimal conditions for practice and performance.

Thermal imaging cameras reveal temperature changes associated with energy work and intuitive healing practices. These objective measurements support subjective reports of energy transfer and manipulation during therapeutic sessions.

Blood chemistry analysis shows measurable changes in hormone levels and neurotransmitter activity during intuitive states. Regular sampling helps identify biochemical markers associated with enhanced intuitive function.

Motion capture technology records subtle physical responses to intuitive information. Advanced systems detect micro-movements that often precede conscious recognition of significant data, providing evidence of embodied cognition.

Sound analysis equipment measures voice pattern changes during intuitive communication. Sophisticated software identifies subtle shifts in tone, rhythm, and frequency that correlate with accurate intuitive transmission.

Light detection systems track subtle photon emissions from biological systems during intuitive interactions. These measurements support theories about biofield communication and energy exchange between organisms.

Magnetic resonance spectroscopy reveals metabolic changes in brain tissue during intuitive processing. Detailed chemical analysis helps identify specific neural mechanisms involved in intuitive perception.

Time-lapse photography captures subtle physical changes during extended intuitive sessions. Frame-by-frame analysis reveals patterns invisible to regular observation, supporting claims of energy-based phenomena.

Gas chromatography detects chemical changes in the local environment during intuitive work. Precise atmospheric analysis helps identify potential molecular mechanisms of information transfer.

Quantum measurement devices explore potential subatomic aspects of intuitive phenomena. Advanced equipment tests theories about quantum entanglement and non-local communication in intuitive processes.

Computer-based testing systems provide standardized assessment of intuitive accuracy. Sophisticated programs generate random targets and track hit rates across large numbers of trials, producing statistically significant results.

Network analysis tools measure patterns of information flow during group intuitive activities. Complex algorithms reveal emerging properties in collective intuitive processes, supporting theories of shared consciousness.

Biofeedback equipment enables real-time monitoring of physiological states during intuitive practice. Immediate feedback helps practitioners optimize their internal conditions for enhanced performance.

Virtual reality systems create controlled environments for testing intuitive capabilities. Programmable scenarios allow systematic investigation of various factors affecting intuitive function.

Data integration platforms combine multiple measurement streams into comprehensive analysis packages. Advanced software synthesizes diverse inputs to reveal complex patterns in intuitive phenomena.

These scientific tools provide essential validation for intuitive development practices while advancing our understanding of underlying mechanisms. Continued technological innovation promises even more precise measurement capabilities in the future. However, practitioners should remember that tools support but cannot replace direct experiential learning in developing intuitive capabilities.

Experiential Documentation

Maintaining accurate records of intuitive experiences forms a crucial foundation for systematic development and validation. Through careful documentation, practitioners create valuable datasets that support both personal growth and broader understanding of intuitive phenomena.

Maria, a clinical psychologist, transformed her intuitive practice through rigorous documentation. By recording detailed observations of her experiences over three years, she identified subtle patterns that significantly improved her accuracy. Her systematic approach not only enhanced her professional work but also provided valuable research data for her colleagues.

Daily journaling serves as the cornerstone of experiential documentation. Practitioners record immediate impressions, physical sensations, emotional responses, and subsequent validations. These entries capture both successes and apparent failures, creating comprehensive learning opportunities.

Time-stamped entries prove particularly valuable for tracking precognitive experiences. Recording impressions before events occur eliminates memory bias and provides clear evidence of predictive accuracy. This practice builds confidence while maintaining honest assessment.

Environmental conditions significantly influence intuitive reception. Detailed notes about temperature, weather, electromagnetic fields, and local events help identify optimal circumstances for practice. This information supports the creation of effective training protocols.

Physical sensations often accompany intuitive insights. Documenting specific bodily responses - tingling, temperature changes, muscle tensions - helps practitioners recognize reliable personal indicators. These somatic markers become valuable guidance tools.

Emotional states correlate strongly with intuitive accuracy. Regular mood tracking reveals personal patterns that enhance or inhibit clear reception. Understanding these emotional influences helps practitioners optimize their practice conditions.

Dream records provide essential data about subconscious processing. Detailed morning notes capture symbolic patterns and precognitive elements that might otherwise be lost. These records often reveal deeper aspects of intuitive development.

Relationship dynamics frequently trigger intuitive experiences. Documenting interactions, impressions, and outcomes helps identify patterns in interpersonal intuition. This information proves valuable for both personal and professional relationships.

Energy perception experiences require particularly careful documentation. Practitioners record subtle sensations, visual impressions, and apparent field effects during energy work. These observations support development of reliable techniques.

Validation protocols form an essential part of documentation practice. Practitioners maintain clear records of how intuitive impressions align with actual events. This systematic verification prevents self-deception and builds genuine confidence.

Photography supplements written records for visual phenomena. Images capture physical changes, energy effects, and environmental conditions that might be difficult to describe in words. This visual documentation provides valuable reference material.

Audio recordings preserve verbal descriptions of immediate experiences. Speaking observations aloud often captures details that might be lost in written notes. These recordings prove particularly valuable during intensive practice sessions.

Video documentation helps track physical responses and environmental interactions. Recording practice sessions reveals subtle patterns often missed in real-time observation. This footage provides valuable feedback for technique refinement.

Quantitative measurements add objective data to subjective experiences. Recording times, distances, frequencies, and other measurable factors helps identify significant patterns. This numerical information supports scientific analysis.

Computer databases organize documentation for effective analysis. Digital platforms enable quick searching, pattern recognition, and data correlation across multiple experiences. This systematic organization reveals insights that might otherwise remain hidden.

Group experiences require coordinated documentation efforts. Multiple observers record their impressions of shared events, providing valuable cross-validation data. These collective records help distinguish personal from universal patterns.

Professional applications demand particularly rigorous documentation. Practitioners maintain detailed case records that meet clinical or research standards. This professional-grade documentation supports broader acceptance of intuitive practices.

Long-term tracking reveals developmental patterns that might be missed in daily notes. Regular review of accumulated records helps practitioners recognize gradual changes and significant transitions. This broader perspective supports continued growth.

Protection protocols include documentation of energetic interactions and boundary issues. Practitioners record techniques that prove effective for maintaining healthy energy fields. These notes help prevent problems during intensive practice periods.

The discipline of consistent documentation often challenges practitioners initially. However, the long-term benefits of systematic recording far outweigh the effort required. Clear records provide both practical guidance and scientific validation for intuitive development.

Success Metrics

Measuring success in intuitive development requires carefully defined metrics that balance quantitative data with qualitative experience. Through systematic evaluation of multiple factors, practitioners can track their progress and validate their growing capabilities.

Sarah, a business consultant, transformed her professional practice by implementing clear success metrics for her intuitive work. Initially skeptical of subjective measurements, she developed a comprehensive system that combined numerical accuracy rates with qualitative assessments. Her approach not only improved her performance but also enhanced client confidence in her services.

Accuracy rates provide fundamental baseline measurements. Practitioners track the percentage of correct intuitive impressions against total attempts, establishing clear performance benchmarks. Regular monitoring of these rates reveals developmental trends and areas needing attention.

Response time measurements indicate growing proficiency. As practitioners develop their abilities, the gap between receiving intuitive information and conscious recognition typically decreases. This improved processing speed reflects enhanced neural integration.

Consistency levels demonstrate reliable skill development. Practitioners monitor their performance across different conditions and circumstances, working to maintain stable accuracy regardless of external factors. This reliability metric proves particularly important for professional applications.

Clarity scores reflect the precision of received information. Practitioners rate the detail and specificity of their intuitive impressions, tracking improvements in signal quality over time. These measurements help identify optimal reception conditions.

Validation speed indicates growing confidence in intuitive signals. As practitioners develop trust in their abilities, they act more quickly on received information. This metric balances against accuracy rates to ensure quality maintenance.

Energy efficiency measurements track sustainable practice development. Practitioners monitor their fatigue levels and recovery times during intensive work, optimizing their energy management strategies. This sustainability metric supports long-term progress.

Integration levels reveal how effectively practitioners combine intuitive information with analytical thinking. Success metrics include assessment of balanced decision-making processes that utilize both cognitive modes. This integration supports practical applications.

Client satisfaction rates provide external validation for professional practitioners. Systematic feedback collection helps identify areas of strength and opportunities for improvement. These assessments contribute to service refinement and business development.

Physical wellness indicators track the body's response to intensive practice. Regular monitoring of health metrics ensures sustainable development without adverse effects. This attention to physical impact supports healthy progression.

Emotional stability measurements assess psychological balance during development. Practitioners track their emotional responses and regulation capabilities as sensitivity increases. These metrics help maintain healthy boundaries and personal well-being.

Financial returns offer practical success metrics for professional practitioners. Tracking income generation and client retention provides concrete validation of service value. These business metrics support sustainable practice development.

Relationship quality indicators reveal social integration success. Practitioners monitor how their developing abilities affect personal and professional relationships. These metrics help optimize communication and boundary management.

Professional recognition provides external validation metrics. Achievement of certifications, peer acknowledgment, and industry standing indicate successful integration of intuitive skills. These credentials support broader acceptance and application.

Research participation generates scientific validation metrics. Involvement in controlled studies and experimental protocols produces documented evidence of intuitive capabilities. These contributions advance field understanding while validating personal development.

Teaching effectiveness measures the ability to transmit knowledge and skills. Practitioners who instruct others track student progress and implementation success. These educational metrics support protocol refinement and field development.

Innovation rates indicate advancing mastery through new applications. Practitioners monitor their development of novel techniques and approaches. These creativity metrics reveal growing sophistication in intuitive work.

Documentation quality provides meta-metrics for development assessment. Regular evaluation of record-keeping practices ensures reliable data for progress tracking. This systematic approach supports continuous improvement.

Community impact measurements track broader influence of intuitive work. Practitioners monitor how their activities affect local and professional communities. These social metrics reveal expanding reach and influence.

Long-term tracking reveals developmental patterns that might be missed in daily assessment. Regular review of accumulated metrics helps practitioners recognize significant transitions and achievements. This comprehensive evaluation supports continued growth while maintaining practical focus on measurable outcomes.

Real-World Application Testing

Testing intuitive abilities in real-world situations provides essential validation and practical experience for developing practitioners. The structured application of intuitive skills across diverse scenarios builds both confidence and competence while generating valuable performance data.

Marcus, a former skeptic turned researcher, discovered the power of real-world testing through a carefully designed year-long study. He began with simple exercises in public spaces, progressing to more complex challenges that demonstrated remarkable accuracy rates. His systematic approach transformed academic understanding of practical intuitive development.

Street testing offers immediate feedback for basic intuitive skills. Practitioners predict immediate events in public settings, such as who will enter a building next or which direction someone will turn. These spontaneous exercises build rapid validation capabilities.

Business environments present complex testing opportunities. Practitioners assess potential outcomes of meetings, negotiations, and market changes. These professional applications generate documented results while providing valuable service.

Medical settings enable testing of health-related intuition. Under appropriate supervision, practitioners offer impressions about patient conditions and treatment responses. These controlled situations provide immediate verification from medical professionals.

Crime investigation work tests advanced intuitive capabilities. Qualified practitioners assist law enforcement agencies with specific cases, generating verifiable results. These high-stakes applications demand rigorous documentation and validation.

Financial markets provide continuous testing opportunities. Practitioners predict market movements and investment outcomes, creating clear numerical validation of their accuracy. These applications generate precise performance metrics.

Sports events offer dynamic testing environments. Practitioners predict game outcomes and specific plays, receiving immediate feedback on their impressions. These recreational applications build confidence through regular validation.

Emergency services work tests rapid intuitive response. Trained practitioners assist first responders in time-critical situations, providing potentially valuable additional information. These high-pressure applications demand exceptional accuracy.

Environmental prediction tests connection with natural systems. Practitioners forecast weather changes and natural events, receiving clear validation through actual outcomes. These applications develop broader awareness of natural patterns.

Technical troubleshooting tests practical problem-solving abilities. Practitioners identify equipment issues and potential solutions, generating immediate verification of their impressions. These applications demonstrate practical value in everyday situations.

Relationship counseling tests interpersonal intuition. Qualified practitioners assess relationship dynamics and potential interventions, receiving feedback through client outcomes. These applications require exceptional ethical awareness.

Educational settings test teaching and learning applications. Practitioners identify student needs and effective approaches, validating their impressions through academic results. These applications support improved educational outcomes.

Agricultural applications test connection with biological systems. Practitioners assess crop conditions and optimal timing for various activities, receiving validation through harvest results. These applications demonstrate practical value in essential industries.

Creative projects test intuitive guidance in artistic expression. Practitioners follow intuitive impulses in creating works of art, receiving validation through audience response. These applications develop trust in creative inspiration.

Scientific research tests precise observation abilities. Practitioners identify promising research directions and potential breakthrough areas, receiving validation through experimental results. These applications advance scientific understanding.

Community development work tests social intuition. Practitioners assess group dynamics and potential interventions, receiving validation through community outcomes. These applications support positive social change.

Personal development coaching tests transformation potential. Practitioners guide individual growth processes, receiving validation through client progress. These applications demonstrate practical value in human development.

Real estate work tests property assessment abilities. Practitioners evaluate properties and market conditions, receiving validation through transaction outcomes. These applications generate clear financial metrics.

Transportation planning tests traffic pattern prediction. Practitioners assess optimal routes and timing, receiving immediate validation through travel outcomes. These applications demonstrate practical value in daily life.

The systematic testing of intuitive abilities in real-world situations provides essential feedback for continued development. Each application area offers unique challenges and validation opportunities, contributing to comprehensive skill development. Through careful documentation and analysis of these experiences, practitioners build both capability and credibility in their chosen fields of application.

Protocol Refinement Processes

Systematic refinement of intuitive protocols ensures continuous improvement and adaptation to changing conditions. Through careful analysis and incremental adjustments, practitioners develop increasingly effective methods for accessing and applying their intuitive abilities.

Lisa, a research psychologist, revolutionized her department's approach to protocol development through innovative refinement techniques. Over three years, she documented subtle improvements that transformed basic exercises into sophisticated training methods. Her systematic approach not only enhanced individual results but also established new standards for intuitive development programs.

Regular performance reviews identify areas needing adjustment in existing protocols. Practitioners analyze success rates across different conditions and circumstances, pinpointing specific elements that affect outcomes. This detailed examination reveals opportunities for targeted improvements.

Environmental factor analysis guides protocol modification. Careful tracking of physical conditions during practice sessions helps optimize training environments. These refinements enhance reception clarity and consistency.

Timing adjustments often yield significant improvements. Practitioners experiment with session duration and frequency, identifying optimal patterns for sustained development. These schedule refinements support efficient skill building while preventing burnout.

Energy management protocols evolve through practical experience. Practitioners modify their approaches based on observed physical and mental effects, developing sustainable practices that support long-term growth. These adjustments ensure healthy progression.

Feedback integration systems improve through iterative development. Practitioners refine their methods for recognizing and interpreting intuitive signals, creating increasingly accurate response patterns. These improvements enhance overall performance.

Protection protocols strengthen through systematic testing. Practitioners adjust their energetic boundaries and shielding techniques based on real-world challenges. These refinements support safe practice in demanding situations.

Documentation methods evolve to capture more relevant data. Practitioners modify their recording systems to track newly recognized factors and correlations. These improvements support more effective analysis and development.

Validation procedures strengthen through practical application. Practitioners refine their methods for confirming intuitive impressions, developing more reliable verification systems. These improvements build confidence and credibility.

Integration techniques advance through experiential learning. Practitioners adjust their approaches for combining intuitive information with analytical thinking, creating more effective decision-making processes. These refinements enhance practical applications.

Teaching protocols improve through student feedback. Instructors modify their methods based on observed learning patterns and outcomes. These adjustments enhance knowledge transfer and skill development.

Research protocols evolve through experimental results. Scientists refine their methods for studying intuitive phenomena, developing more effective investigation techniques. These improvements advance field understanding.

Professional application protocols strengthen through client response. Practitioners adjust their service delivery methods based on practical outcomes and feedback. These refinements enhance client satisfaction and results.

Group practice protocols develop through collective experience. Facilitators modify their approaches based on observed group dynamics and learning patterns. These improvements support more effective collective development.

Emergency response protocols refine through real-world application. Practitioners adjust their methods for crisis situations based on actual outcomes. These improvements enhance reliability under pressure.

Remote perception protocols evolve through distance testing. Practitioners modify their techniques for non-local sensing based on validated results. These refinements expand practical applications.

Healing protocols strengthen through documented outcomes. Practitioners adjust their approaches based on observed therapeutic effects and client recovery patterns. These improvements enhance treatment effectiveness.

Communication protocols develop through practical dialogue. Practitioners refine their methods for sharing intuitive information with others, creating clearer understanding. These adjustments support better collaboration.

Quality control protocols evolve through systematic assessment. Practitioners modify their evaluation methods based on observed performance patterns. These improvements maintain high standards while supporting growth.

The ongoing refinement of intuitive protocols represents a dynamic process of continuous improvement. Each adjustment, whether minor or significant, contributes to the development of more effective practices. Through careful attention to outcomes and systematic modification of approaches, practitioners create increasingly sophisticated methods for accessing and applying intuitive abilities. This evolutionary process ensures that protocols remain relevant and effective while adapting to advancing understanding of intuitive development.

Chapter 6: Breaking Free from Control Systems

Identifying External Influences

External influences significantly impact intuitive perception and development, requiring careful identification and management for optimal results. Understanding these influences enables practitioners to maintain clarity and accuracy while navigating complex environments.

David, a corporate consultant, discovered the profound effect of external influences during a high-stakes merger negotiation. His initial intuitive impressions seemed contradictory until he recognized the competing pressures from various stakeholders. By methodically identifying and accounting for these external factors, he successfully guided the process to a beneficial conclusion.

Environmental factors create immediate impacts on intuitive reception. Electronic interference, electromagnetic fields, and ambient noise levels affect signal clarity. Practitioners learn to recognize and compensate for these physical influences through systematic observation and documentation.

Social dynamics generate powerful effects on intuitive perception. Group emotions, collective expectations, and interpersonal tensions create complex fields of influence. Understanding these social currents helps practitioners maintain clear reception in challenging situations.

Cultural beliefs shape interpretation of intuitive information. Societal norms, religious perspectives, and traditional viewpoints color how practitioners process their impressions. Awareness of these cultural filters enables more objective understanding.

Professional pressures affect intuitive accuracy. Workplace expectations, client demands, and career considerations can distort perception. Recognition of these influences supports maintained integrity in business applications.

Media exposure creates pervasive background effects. News cycles, social media, and entertainment content generate emotional atmospheres that impact intuitive clarity. Practitioners develop strategies for maintaining clear perception amid information saturation.

Political environments generate strong influential fields. Public opinions, policy debates, and power dynamics create complex interference patterns. Understanding these influences helps practitioners navigate sensitive situations.

Economic conditions affect collective consciousness. Market forces, financial pressures, and resource concerns generate powerful currents of influence. Recognition of these factors supports accurate interpretation of business-related impressions.

Weather patterns impact intuitive reception. Atmospheric conditions, seasonal changes, and natural cycles create varying effects on perception. Practitioners learn to adjust for these environmental influences.

Geographic locations carry distinct energetic signatures. Different places generate unique fields of influence based on history, population, and natural features. Understanding these spatial effects helps practitioners maintain consistent performance across locations.

Time periods hold specific influential patterns. Historical events, cultural memories, and collective anticipation create temporal effects on perception. Recognition of these time-based influences supports accurate interpretation.

Personal relationships generate significant impacts. Family dynamics, friendship bonds, and romantic connections create powerful fields of influence. Practitioners develop awareness of these intimate effects on their perception.

Health conditions affect receptive clarity. Physical wellness, emotional balance, and mental state impact intuitive accuracy. Understanding these personal influences enables appropriate adjustments.

Educational background shapes interpretive frameworks. Academic training, professional expertise, and learned patterns influence how practitioners process information. Awareness of these cognitive filters supports clearer perception.

Technological environments create modern challenges. Digital devices, virtual interactions, and automated systems generate novel fields of influence. Practitioners develop strategies for maintaining clarity in tech-saturated settings.

Natural cycles impact intuitive reception. Circadian rhythms, lunar phases, and seasonal patterns affect perceptive abilities. Understanding these natural influences helps optimize practice timing.

Global events generate widespread effects. International developments, mass movements, and planetary conditions create far-reaching influences. Recognition of these macro factors supports accurate interpretation of broader patterns.

Local community dynamics affect daily practice. Neighborhood conditions, regional events, and community attitudes create immediate fields of influence. Practitioners learn to navigate these proximate effects while maintaining clear perception.

Professional networks generate field-specific influences. Industry trends, peer expectations, and professional standards affect how practitioners apply their abilities. Understanding these specialized impacts supports effective service delivery.

Through systematic identification and understanding of external influences, practitioners develop increasingly sophisticated strategies for maintaining clear intuitive perception. This awareness enables more accurate reception and interpretation while supporting sustained development of reliable abilities. The skilled practitioner learns to navigate these various fields of influence while maintaining focus on essential information.

Reclaiming Intuitive Authority

Intuitive authority emerges through dedicated practice and personal validation, establishing a foundation of trust in one's natural perceptive abilities. The process of reclaiming this innate capacity involves overcoming societal conditioning and reconnecting with internal wisdom.

Sarah, a corporate executive, discovered her path to intuitive authority during a critical business decision. Despite external pressure to follow conventional analysis, she trusted her deep inner knowing, which led to an unprecedented success. Her experience transformed not only her career but also inspired others to trust their intuitive guidance.

Early life experiences often suppress natural intuitive abilities. Cultural messaging, educational systems, and social expectations can create barriers between individuals and their innate wisdom. Recognizing these influences marks the first step toward reclaiming intuitive authority.

Personal validation builds through direct experience. Each confirmed intuitive impression strengthens trust in these natural abilities. Systematic documentation of successful insights creates a foundation of confidence.

Professional accomplishments demonstrate practical value. Applying intuitive guidance in work situations generates tangible results. These successes establish credibility while encouraging further development.

Family dynamics often challenge intuitive authority. Ancestral patterns and childhood conditioning may resist this reconnection process. Working through these layers supports fuller access to natural abilities.

Scientific understanding supports intuitive development. Research in neuroplasticity and consciousness studies validates the reality of intuitive perception. This knowledge helps overcome skepticism while building confidence.

Creative expression facilitates intuitive reconnection. Artistic activities bypass analytical resistance, allowing natural abilities to emerge. These experiences strengthen trust in non-linear perception.

Physical wellness enhances intuitive clarity. Body awareness and energetic balance support stronger connection with internal wisdom. Regular self-care practices maintain optimal receptivity.

Emotional intelligence complements intuitive authority. Understanding personal feelings and others' emotions strengthens intuitive accuracy. This emotional literacy supports better interpretation of intuitive impressions.

Mental clarity supports reliable reception. Regular meditation and mindfulness practices reduce internal noise. These techniques enhance discrimination between true intuition and mental chatter.

Environmental awareness affects intuitive strength. Connection with nature and sensitivity to surroundings enhance perceptive abilities. This ecological consciousness supports broader intuitive understanding.

Professional boundaries protect intuitive clarity. Clear limits and ethical guidelines maintain energetic integrity. These boundaries support sustainable practice while building credibility.

Personal relationships benefit from intuitive authority. Improved understanding and communication enhance connections with others. These strengthened relationships validate intuitive guidance.

Social change occurs through collective intuitive awakening. Communities benefit when individuals reclaim their natural wisdom. This expanded awareness supports positive cultural evolution.

Leadership improves through intuitive integration. Decision-making becomes more effective when combining analysis with intuition. This balanced approach generates better outcomes.

Educational systems evolve through intuitive recognition. Learning environments improve when incorporating natural knowing. This integration supports fuller human development.

Healthcare advances through intuitive awareness. Treatment becomes more effective when considering whole-person wisdom. This comprehensive approach enhances healing outcomes.

Business success increases with intuitive guidance. Strategic decisions improve when incorporating natural knowing. This balanced perspective generates sustainable growth.

Scientific discovery accelerates through intuitive insight. Research breakthroughs often follow intuitive leads. This integration of approaches advances human knowledge.

Global challenges require intuitive wisdom. Complex problems need solutions incorporating natural knowing. This expanded awareness supports effective responses to planetary issues.

The process of reclaiming intuitive authority represents a fundamental shift in human consciousness. As individuals reconnect with their natural wisdom, they contribute to a broader awakening of collective awareness. This development supports more effective decision-making across all areas of life while fostering positive social evolution. Through consistent practice and validation, practitioners establish reliable access to their intuitive abilities, creating positive change in both personal and professional spheres.

Environmental Optimization

Creating optimal conditions for intuitive development requires careful attention to both physical and energetic environments. The subtle interplay between space, energy, and consciousness significantly impacts the quality of intuitive reception and interpretation.

Michael, a research scientist, transformed his laboratory into a model of environmental optimization. By systematically adjusting lighting, sound, and electromagnetic fields, he documented a 40% improvement in experimental accuracy. His groundbreaking work demonstrated the crucial role of environmental factors in enhancing intuitive abilities.

Physical space arrangement directly affects intuitive clarity. Room layout, furniture placement, and object positioning create energy flows that either support or hinder perception. Strategic organization of space enhances receptivity while minimizing interference.

Natural light quality influences receptive ability. Sunlight exposure, window placement, and artificial lighting choices impact energetic balance. Proper lighting design supports sustained practice while reducing eye strain.

Sound management shapes perceptive clarity. Ambient noise levels, acoustic treatments, and background sounds affect concentration. Careful audio environment design enhances focus while reducing distraction.

Air quality affects mental clarity. Ventilation systems, plant presence, and air purification methods impact cognitive function. Clean air supports optimal brain performance and intuitive reception.

Temperature regulation influences comfort levels. Thermal balance, air circulation, and humidity control affect physical ease. Comfortable conditions enable longer practice sessions with better results.

Electromagnetic field management ensures clear reception. Electronic device placement, wiring configuration, and shielding techniques reduce interference. Proper management of these fields supports more accurate perception.

Color selection impacts psychological state. Wall colors, fabric choices, and decorative elements affect mood and energy. Thoughtful color schemes support balanced practice environments.

Natural elements enhance energetic flow. Plants, water features, and organic materials create harmonious spaces. These elements support connection with natural rhythms and patterns.

Workspace organization affects mental focus. Desktop arrangement, storage solutions, and tool placement impact efficiency. Clear organization supports undistracted practice sessions.

Sacred space creation supports deeper connection. Altar areas, meditation corners, and contemplative zones enhance practice quality. These dedicated spaces facilitate regular development work.

Seasonal adjustments maintain optimal conditions. Environmental modifications, schedule changes, and practice adaptations follow natural cycles. These adjustments support year-round development.

Group space design facilitates collective work. Seating arrangements, energy flow patterns, and interaction zones support shared experience. Effective design enhances group practice sessions.

Professional environment optimization supports practical application. Office layout, meeting space design, and work area arrangement affect performance. These improvements enhance business applications.

Home practice space development enables consistent growth. Personal area design, family space integration, and private zone creation support daily practice. These arrangements facilitate regular development.

Travel adaptation techniques maintain practice quality. Portable tools, space clearing methods, and temporary arrangement skills support mobility. These strategies enable consistent practice while traveling.

Emergency backup systems ensure continued practice. Alternative power sources, protective shields, and backup locations support continuation during disruptions. These preparations maintain development momentum.

Digital space management supports modern practice. Screen positioning, device arrangement, and virtual environment design affect online work. These considerations enable effective remote practice.

Community space enhancement supports collective growth. Shared facility design, public area arrangement, and group space optimization benefit many practitioners. These improvements facilitate broader development.

Through systematic attention to environmental factors, practitioners create spaces that enhance intuitive development while supporting sustained practice. These optimized environments enable clearer reception, more accurate interpretation, and faster skill development. Regular assessment and adjustment of environmental conditions ensure continued effectiveness while adapting to changing needs and circumstances.

www.ingramcontent.com/pod-product-compliance
Lightning Source LLC
LaVergne TN
LVHW022113200926
848481LV00003B/1160